# SEND SOMETHING BEAUTIFUL

# SEND SOMETHING BEAUTIFUL

Fold, pull, print, cut and turn paper into collectible keepsakes and memorable mail

EMILY HOGARTH

APPLE

A QUINTET BOOK

First published in the UK in 2014 by Apple Press
74-77 White Lion Street,
London N1 9PF
United Kingdom

www.apple-press.com

Copyright © 2014 Quintet Publishing Limited

ISBN: 978-1-84543-548-6
QTT.PBO

This book was conceived, designed and
produced by Quintet Publishing Limited
4th Floor, Sheridan House
114-116 Western Road
Hove BN3 1DD
United Kingdom

Project Designers: Sarah Dennis, Ivana Charvatova,
Otokar Charvat, Lynn Hatzius, Emily Hogarth, Emily
Isabella, Freya Lines, Marthe Van Herk, Mr. Yen
Designer: Tania Gomes
Photographers: Lydia Evans & Mark Hudson
Art Director: Michael Charles
Editorial Director: Emma Bastow
Publisher: Mark Searle
Editorial Assistant: Ella Lines
Publishing Assistant: Alice Sambrook

Manufactured in China by 1010 Printing
International Ltd.

9 8 7 6 5 4 3 2 1

# Contents

# Project Selector

**Page 73** Paper Stamp

**Page 78** Botanical Paper-Cut Card

**Page 83** Message Card

**Page 86** Flower Card

**Page 91** Bird Pop-Up Card

**Page 94** Flower Twist Card

**Page 99** Secret Message Petal Card

**Page 102** Pigeon Postcard

**Page 108** Sending Spring

**Page 113** Blue Ribbon Thank You

**Page 116** Floral Border Notecard

**Page 121** Patterned Gatefold Card

**Page 124** Whale Card

**Page 129** Parrots

# INTRODUCTION

In this digital age, a simple handmade card, postcard, invitation or crafted gift can often mean more than a thousand emails or texts. As our communications with one another become more and more digital, there is a growing appreciation for sending notes and gifts by post. Imagine receiving a hand-crafted card that has been designed especially for you – perhaps with your name or a special motif incorporated into the artistry. A composite postcard sent in instalments that completes a picture over time, hand-printed gift wrap, or a delicate paper-cut card are all delightful to receive. It's hard to resist such attention to detail, originality, hand-crafted skill and old-school charm. The art of creating and sending something beautiful can be a real joy and this book shows you how.

Whether you are looking for new ways to correspond, want a change from digital technology, or just love crafting with paper, this book is for you! Complete with 25 projects that will ignite your creativity, these projects and tutorials are perfect for inspiring you to send gifts by post again! So make someone's day and send something beautiful!

## EMILY HOGARTH

# Tools & materials

One of the best things about papercrafts is that you don't need a lot of materials to get started. You can create a lovely greetings card with just a piece of thin card or paper and a pen, but to make something really special, there are a few more tools you might like to use.

**Pencil**  Every crafter needs a pencil and sharpener to draw designs. A medium-grade pencil such as an HB is recommended, as it produces a crisp fine line and can be easily erased.

**Eraser**  It is rare to find artists who don't need to redraw their designs a few times to get it just right. An eraser will help you get rid of any unwanted pencil marks and can be used to create your own stamps (see page 21).

**Adhesives**  Use different types of adhesives for your projects. Double-sided tape is a very good option because it isn't messy and sticks well to paper. Spray adhesives are also good, as they have less moisture than white glue – too much moisture can warp paper. Glue sticks are another good adhesive for paper projects but may be less tacky than other glues. Superglue can also work well, but use it cautiously and sparingly.

**Low-tack tape**  Low-tack tape is great for attaching templates to paper. Scotch tape and masking tape are best, but press down lightly to avoid tearing the paper. Test tape on a scrap of paper before you begin.

**Scissors**  Keep a large pair of scissors for general cutting and a small pair (such as embroidery scissors) for delicate paper-cutting work. Make sure they are comfortable to hold – the last thing you want is sore hands.

**Craft knife**  A hand-held craft knife with replaceable blades is essential for creating small, intricate cuts. Always make sure you have a stock of new blades, as you will need to change it often to ensure neat cuts.

**Metal ruler** Always use a metal ruler for cutting straight edges with a craft knife, as the knife can slip and cut into plastic or wood rulers.

**Cutting mat** A self-healing cutting mat protects your tabletop and also prevents your craft knife from slipping. Cutting mats are available in many sizes and often feature a ruled grid, which is helpful for lining up papers.

**Bone folder** This is a tool that helps you create smooth, crisp creases and folds. It isn't essential but can be a very useful tool.

**Needle and thread** You can use a needle to pierce small holes in paper, and thread is very handy for hanging up your paper-cutting projects.

**Brass paper fasteners** These can be found in most stationery shops and are great tools for adding hinged, moving parts to projects, such as the Parrots card on page 129.

**Tracing paper and carbon paper** Tracing paper is transparent and useful for copying templates out of a book and onto paper. Carbon paper also helps when transferring an image onto paper because it has ink on one side that transfers onto paper when drawn on the back. See page 15 for how to use tracing and carbon paper.

**Paints or coloured pencils** Use coloured pencils or paints to give your projects extra detail.

**Ink pads** Ink pads are available in arts and crafts shops in a wide variety of colours. Use them for inking carved rubber stamps to create beautiful patterns for gift wrap and cards.

**Carving tools** To create your own stamps, you will need a simple lino carving kit (available from craft shops). The kits usually include a handle with a few different carving nibs – tools that allow you to carve out designs on rubber and lino to create your own stamps (see page 21).

# Getting Started

A nyone can make beautiful papercrafts. Getting started is simple and this brief introductory advice is all you need to start cutting, gluing and sending something beautiful.

## Choosing Paper

Paper is the main material used for all the projects in this book – I think it is safe to say it is the main component in card craft projects! There are so many different options when it comes to paper – from weight and colour, to texture and pattern – that it is worth considering what you are going to use before starting your project.

There are no rules to creating your own paper project and I suggest trying different paper. However, some types of paper work better than others for certain projects. For example, when creating a project that requires folding the paper more than once (such as the Origami Hearts on page 41) a thin paper is definitely better. If the paper is too thick, it is hard to fold again and again. Therefore I suggest using origami-style paper for these projects, as it is designed for folding more than once. If your project has a lot of small details to cut out using a craft knife, you also don't want a very thick paper, as those small sections would be very hard to cut out. On the other hand, when gluing a paper-cut design onto a card, thick, heavy paper is perfect to use for the base. That way your card will be nice and strong and stand up well.

Different types of paper can also add different effects to your projects. A beautiful handmade paper has a soft quality that would look lovely in the Hanging Notes project on page 67. Tissue paper and crepe paper are also very useful to have around. These thin papers can often look almost translucent, giving them a totally different feel. Crepe paper is a form of tissue paper that has been treated to create tiny gatherings over the paper's surface to give it a bumpy texture. Also, don't forget about patterned paper which is a great way to add another dimension to your work. Shop-bought patterned paper is also a good option. Think about using materials that you already have around the house, such as old newspapers, sheets of music, gift wrap, etc.

Paper is described in different ways, but the most common distinction is by weight. Generally, paper is measured in grams per square metre (gsm). Printer paper is roughly 80 gsm while artists' drawing paper is roughly 150 gsm. In the United States, however, paper weight is measured in pounds per ream. A ream is usually 500 sheets, so the heavier the ream, the thicker the paper. For example, printer paper is roughly 100 lb per ream while artists' drawing paper is roughly 220 lb per ream.

With some experimentation and exploring options in craft shops, you will get a feel for what paper you like. You will begin to know what weight works well for paper cutting and folding and which colours go nicely together. This all comes with time, but in the beginning, just get started and try out lots of different types of paper. We suggest what sorts of paper work well for most of the projects in this book, but feel free to use others as well.

# Paper Cutting

You will need to know a few cutting techniques for some of the projects in this book. There are more details about paper cutting on page 24, but here is a quick overview on how to use scissors and a craft knife to create sharp, clean cuts.

**Scissors**  Scissors come in different shapes and sizes, and I think it is always best to have a couple of different sizes around when working. Larger scissors are great for cutting big sheets of paper and large shapes quickly and easily whereas small scissors are best used for the small, intricate details. The easiest way to cut with scissors is by sitting down, resting your elbows on a table and holding a piece of paper in front of you at eye height. Hold the scissors in one hand and use your other hand to guide the paper into the blades. Try to keep the hand that is holding the scissors fairly steady, and try not to let the blades of your scissors close fully – this will give you a smoother finish.

Using scissors to cut small, detailed areas within a design is tricky. Do these first so that if you make a mistake, you can start again easily without having wasted any time on the other sections. First pierce a small hole with the tip of the scissors in the area you are going to remove and make a small snip. Once you have this initial opening, you can ease the scissors in and continue to cut.

**Craft knife**  A craft knife, or scalpel, is a very popular choice for papercrafts (especially paper cutting), as it allows you to make much smaller, more accurate cuts.

There are a few things to consider before starting with your knife:

- Buy a craft knife that is comfortable to hold. They come in a wide variety of shapes and sizes, so shop around and see what works for you.

- Buy a craft knife that has replaceable blades or a blade that you can sharpen easily. A sharp blade makes cleaner and more accurate cuts and is less likely to slip and cut you. It is time to change your blade when you feel it resisting the paper and dragging slightly.

- Always use a self-healing cutting mat to protect your work surface and prevent the blade from blunting too quickly.

**Tearing**  This requires no cutting at all. Simply fold the paper in half, press the crease down firmly, and then unfold the paper. Place your left hand to the left of the crease; press down firmly on the paper to hold it in place. Hold the top right-hand corner in your right hand and gently pull down towards yourself. This should give you a nice torn edge. You might find it easier to place your right hand down on the paper and tear with your left – either way works.

**Paper punches**  Paper punches are a great way to cut paper into a specific shape. You can find a wide variety of sizes and shapes in most craft shops.

## SAFETY FIRST

Keep your blades in a safe place – especially your used ones, as they are still very sharp. I find an old Kilner jar with a lid is a good place to store them. When you are not using your blade, make sure you store it with the blade tip covered (or removed) and facing downwards in a container to avoid any accidents.

# Using templates

You will find that a lot of craft books use templates (see page 132–141). These are designed to help you make an accurate copy of the project shown. There are a couple of ways to transfer a template from a book onto paper.

**Photocopying and scanning**  This is the most common technique and this method also allows you to alter the size of the template to suit your needs.

To do so you have to alter the scale of the template. If you want the template to be smaller, then you want the scale to be less than 100 per cent. Alternatively, if you want the template to be larger, then you want the scale to be more than 100 per cent. Once you have copied the template, you can attach it directly to your paper and cut around it.

**Tracing paper**  This method does not require any fancy technology. If the template is shown at 100 per cent, simply place a piece of tracing paper over the template and carefully draw around it using a soft pencil (and remember to include any little details within the design too). Next lay the tracing paper wrong-side up (so the pencil side is on the paper) and draw over your lines again with a harder pencil, such as an HB. The pressure should transfer the pencil marks from your original pencil lines onto the paper. Once you have transferred the design, remove the tracing paper and use the pencil to go over any areas that didn't come out fully.

**Carbon paper**  Carbon paper uses the same principle as tracing paper. It has ink on one side, so that when you draw on the other side, it transfers the ink to your paper. If the template is shown at 100 per cent, place a piece of paper on your work surface and then place a piece of carbon paper on top (ink-side down on the paper). Next lay the template on top and draw over it – your drawn line will transfer to the paper on the bottom. If you can't draw directly onto the template (if it is a book, for example), then trace it first and then place the tracing on top of the carbon paper.

# Papercraft Inspiration

Inspiration can come from anything and anywhere – a beautiful scene, the smell of fresh flowers, or even the packaging in your supermarket. When it comes to papercrafts – especially things you can send – inspiration often comes from the project itself. What occasion is it for? Who is the recipient, and what is his or her personality and character? These questions are a good place to start. It is easy to get caught up in the craft and forget who is going to enjoy it, so when beginning any project, think about its final home and what that person likes.

When seeking inspiration for crafts that you can post, a logical place to start is in the greetings cards section at your local newsagents or gift shop. Look around and see what you are drawn to. It might be the colour, a particular image or the layout of a design. My suggestion for seeking inspiration is to collect items and images that you like, from photographs and colour swatches to flowers and patterned fabric. If you keep them together, you will probably find a common theme: a certain colour that attracts you or a particular subject matter – perhaps you really like cats or dogs.

Finding out what you like, as well as knowing who is going to enjoy your craft, should give you enough inspiration to get started!

# Techniques

Some basic techniques are very useful when you first venture into the creative world of making papercraft projects. This section covers all the basic techniques needed to complete the projects found in this book.

## Folding

Many papercrafts involve some degree of folding. If your project involves a lot of folding, it is important to consider the type of paper you are using. If you are just folding a piece of paper in half to create a card, it is fine to use a heavy-weight paper, however if you want to fold a piece of paper many times and cut into it to create a pattern, a thinner piece of paper is advisable.

There are many ways to fold paper. The simplest and most common method is the single fold (like a card). Another is the accordion fold – where you fold a piece of paper back and forth over itself to create a fan-like appearance. Multi-folding is when you fold a piece of paper into quarters or eighths before cutting into it. The only limit on how many times you fold your paper is its thickness. When cutting into folded designs, remember a few important points:

- Be careful along the folded edge (or edges). This edge holds the paper together, so it will fall apart if you cut away too much of the design. Some templates use a broken line to represent a folded edge, so make sure that the broken line aligns with the fold of the paper so you don't cut through it. As with many paper-cutting techniques, it is always best to start by cutting the smaller details within a design before you cut around the outside edge.

- With multi-fold designs, you have two folded edges to consider. Parts of the design have to be in contact with both of these edges at all times to make sure the design stays intact when you unfold it.

- Avoid unfolding the paper until you have finished cutting. This will keep the paper from slipping out of position while you are cutting.

# Scoring and Indenting

These are terms for folding techniques that are especially useful for thicker cardstock that is hard to fold neatly with just your fingers.

Scoring lightly cuts through the surface of the paper or card, making it easier to fold. To score, place a metal ruler where you would like the fold to be (usually in the centre). Next carefully and gently slide a craft knife along the edge of the ruler. You only want to cut the surface and not all the way through. Don't press too hard! Once you're finished, turn the paper over, fold in half and the scored edge will be on the outside.

Indenting is used more often than scoring since there is no risk of cutting through the paper. This technique uses pressure to indent a line in the paper or card, making it easier to fold. Place a metal ruler along the line you would like to fold, holding a craft knife upside down (or the end of a bone folder). Press the end of the craft knife into the paper along the ruler edge. Unlike scoring, you want to fold the paper in on itself so that the indented crease is on the inside.

These are just some of the basic folding techniques, but they should give you a good starting point to create all the projects in this book.

# Origami

*Origami* is the name for traditional Japanese paper folding. Unlike other paper art forms, origami transforms a single flat sheet of paper into a three-dimensional object using only folding techniques – no gluing, no cutting. There are thousands of books dedicated to this subject alone, but the key principles of this craft are very simple; fold the paper and do not cut.

A couple of key folds are the Valley Fold and the Mountain Fold. The Valley Fold creates a V shape and the Mountain Fold creates a peak resembling an A. After that, follow the instructions to manipulate your piece of paper into shape.

Origami paper comes in a huge variety of beautifully patterned and coloured paper in ready-cut squares. This paper is very thin and holds a nice sharp crease. There is no exact weight of paper that is best for this art form, but shop-bought origami paper always works very well. If this isn't available to you, use writing or photocopy paper. Use a bone folder to create very sharp creases and folds; you can also use paperclips to hold the paper while you fold another section, or tweezers to fold very small sections.

If I can pass on any advice when it comes to origami it is to take your time. Make sure your folds are accurate and line up perfectly (especially in the beginning). If one fold is out of line, it can affect all the other folds. Take your time and be precise.

# Layering and Intercutting

These techniques allow you to add more than one colour to a design and extra depth to your work in the process.

Layering means exactly what it sounds like – laying one piece of paper on top of another to create layers. There is no limit to the amount of layers you can add to a design, but remember that you want to put your project in the post, so too many layers will make it hard to fit in an envelope. One of the great advantages to designing in this way is that if you make a mistake or don't like a section of the design, you can easily redo that layer without having to redo the whole project.

If you want to create depth in your designs, it is a good idea to create a gradation. Start with a lighter colour at the back and add darker shades as you come forwards. For example, if you have yellow at the back, make the next colour orange, then red, maroon and finally dark purple. This will give you a sense of depth in a picture. This is by no means a rule, but it is worth considering when planning your design.

You can also use layers to create backgrounds for paper-cut work. Cut out a solid piece of paper the same size as your paper-cut design in a different colour. Attach it behind your design. This instantly lifts the design.

You can also try intercutting – a technique that involves cutting through two pieces of paper at the same time and then swapping the cut sections. It works best when you use two contrasting colours. Place the papers on top of one another and secure them together using low-tack tape. It is important that the pieces of paper don't move out of place when you are cutting. Start cutting out your design and remember to press slightly harder, as you are cutting through two pieces of paper. Once you have cut your first shape, remove the cut sections and place them safely to one side. Separate the paper and place the cut section back into the opposite piece of paper. Secure back into place using invisible tape. You can repeat this process again and again on the same piece of paper to create some wonderful effects.

# Pop-ups

Pop-up designs are a great way to add a three-dimensional element to your designs. They first appeared in children's books – adding exciting elements to the page and bringing stories to life. Today they are commonly used in the greetings card industry as well as in books.

A pop-up card uses folds, cuts and sometimes extra pieces to make a two-dimensional image three-dimensional. Pop-up cards can often be incredibly complex, and when you open them up, it is magical to watch all the pieces fall into place.

When you first start creating pop-ups, it is a good idea to practise using a medium-weight paper. Once you have the techniques mastered, the best type of paper to use is a thinner, springy cardstock that you can buy at most art and craft shops.

# Paper cutting

Paper cutting is the art of cutting away shapes from a single piece of paper to create a new image. Simply fold a piece of paper and cut away at the edges with a pair of scissors until you can unfold the paper and reveal your delicate, symmetrical paper-cut design.

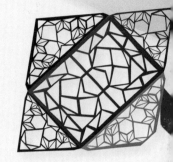

A craft knife, or scalpel, is a popular choice for paper cutters as it lets you achieve small, accurate cuts. You can also create paper cuts with a pair of scissors, but this is more difficult. There are a few things to remember when using a craft knife for paper cutting:

- Hold your craft knife the same way you would hold a pencil at about a 45-degree angle from the paper. When cutting, it is a good idea to pull the blade through the paper towards you, rather than pushing the blade away from you. This gives you more control, which makes it much safer. Use a metal ruler to cut a straight edge. Place the ruler along the line to be cut. Place the fingers of your non-cutting hand onto the ruler, well away from the edge, and hold the ruler in place. Glide your knife down the other edge of the ruler, cutting the paper.
- When cutting a curved edge, take your time! It isn't always easy to get a smooth line, but if you take your time and gently ease the paper around so that your blade is always cutting towards you, you will get a smooth line. Finally, I just want to mention *overcutting* and *undercutting* as you will definitely come across these issues in your projects. Overcutting and undercutting are the terms used when you either cut too far or not far enough. Try to be as accurate as possible, but don't worry too much as it is bound to happen.

# Stamping and Printing

Creating your own stamps is a great way to add a decorative touch to a variety of projects. Start with a carving block – this can be anything from a small household eraser to a potato. As long as you can carve a design out of it and you have something to grip, it can be used. Next you will need some carving tools. You can use a scalpel or knife to cut out simple shapes, but if you want to create a stamp with fine lines and small details, it is worth investing in a lino cutter. Lino cutters can be purchased from most art and craft shops and often come with replaceable nibs so that you can carve a variety of line widths.

To transfer your stamp to your paper, you need inks. You can pick up ink pads in a wide range of colours from your local art and craft shop, and you can even find ink that is suitable for fabric. The possibilities are endless.

Once your stamp is carved, gently press it into an ink pad a couple of times to get even coverage. You don't want too much ink as the design will become smudged, but you also don't want too little. Once you have inked the stamp, turn it over and place the inked side down onto your paper. Gently press on the back. Then carefully remove the stamp in one clean movement to reveal the image.

# Typography

Typography is the art of arranging type so that it is aesthetically pleasing. Typography comprises of the space between letters, the different fonts used, the space between lines, and the size of the letters. There are so many options to choose from.

Calligraphy is a beautiful way to hand-inscribe an envelope and adds a very romantic feel to the overall look. Alternatively, you could use a traditional typewriter to type a letter to create an element of nostalgia in your artwork. Cutting out letters from a newspaper and rearranging them is another creative way to use type. You can even download a variety of fonts – there are so many options, so don't be afraid to get creative!

## PERSONALISED WRITING PAPER

Try creating personalised writing paper with your own initials on it. First draw your initials in reverse onto your block (see page 21). If you are feeling brave, you can create a cursive look (lower case and flowing), or keep things simple with capital letters. Once you have drawn your initials, carve around them, trying to keep the edges of your letters sharp. Once the letters are cut out, you can ink them and press onto the top centre of your writing paper. Voilà – your very own personalised writing paper.

# From Prep to Post

## Formatting letters and postcards

There are formal ways to a write letter, especially when writing a letter for a job application or to someone professional, but in today's society, rules are there to be broken. As long as your letter is addressed to someone and you let them know who it is from (unless it is a secret love affair) then anything goes.

Traditionally, you would start by formatting your letter with your address in the top right-hand corner. Over on the left side you would write the recipient's address (slightly lower than the address on the right). Next, you would write the date (write the month as a word rather than as a number). People's opinions differ over whether the date should be on the right- or the left-hand side but I would normally write it on the right-hand, under my own address. Finally, under the recipient's address on the left-hand side you would write your greeting, this can be either 'Dear Sir/Madam' or you can use their name. Then on a new paragraph starting slightly in from the left you would start writing your letter. On ending your letter you can write 'yours faithfully' if you do not know the name of the recipient or 'yours sincerely' if you do know the recipient. Obviously, if you know the recipient well then you can write anything – love, from, best wishes, etc.

Above is the format of a traditional letter most commonly used today for business correspondents, but it can also be very helpful to include some of these details in your everyday letters too. It is good practice to include your address in the letter either at the top of the page as mentioned above or on the back of the envelope. You would be surprised how many people don't keep address books anymore, so if you are hoping for a response, make sure your address is available.

Postcards are also used today to send people short messages, especially when they are travelling. Usually the back of a postcard is divided into two sections. On the right-hand side you write the name of the recipient and their full address, and you write your note on the left-hand side. Unlike letters that get placed into envelopes, postcards don't use envelopes at all. Your text can be seen be everyone, which is worth remembering if you want to write something private.

However, as I said in the introduction, rules are there to be broken. Today you don't have to be as formal with your letter writing. Think about using old photographs of your loved ones as postcards; write on the back of them and get posting. You don't have to send postcards just when you travel – I always think it is nice to send postcards of where you live as well.

# ENVELOPES

Envelopes are an important part of sending cards and letters, as they are the vehicle in which your words get to their recipient safely. There are many different styles and shapes of envelopes, and you can even make your own. There are so many different types of envelopes that it is almost impossible to list them all. Instead, I will go over a few of the most common.

**Traditional flap envelopes** These come in a wide variety of shapes and sizes but typically they are rectangular or square in shape with triangle or rectangular flaps. The sizes of these flaps can vary, and you can play around with their proportions to get different looks and styles for your own envelope.

**Window envelopes** These envelopes have a small section cut out that is usually replaced with a thin, clear film. This is so that the recipient's address (which has been written on the letter) can be seen through the envelope, which saves you from writing the address again.

**Security envelope** Have you ever noticed that some envelopes are patterned on the inside? Banks use this style of envelope all the time because it is harder to see the contents of the envelope through the pattern. This is a very simple security technique.

**Closing techniques** There are many different ways to close and secure an envelope. Many envelopes have a gummed edge that you moisten to make it tacky before pressing down to secure. Today some envelopes have a self-sealing strip, so you don't have to lick them. There are also envelopes that use metal fasteners through a hole to secure the flap in place. My favourite is the string and button fixture – so simple and yet so pleasing to unwind the string and find your letter inside.

**Decorating your envelope** Traditionally an envelope should have the recipient's address on the front, and this shouldn't be written too large as you need to leave room for a stamp. Stamps are usually placed in the top right-hand corner of the envelope, so avoid writing your address there. I always think it is nice to embellish your envelope a little too. Add some small painted flowers around the address or use some pretty tape. Just make sure you don't add anything to the envelope that might fall off or get caught while in transit.

# Finishing artwork and getting it ready to Post

There are many ways to create your papercrafts so that they can be admired by many and also stay safe until they reach their recipient – whether that is through the post or by hand delivery.

Keep your work flat to prevent damage until you are ready to send it. Also, it is always a good idea to keep your cards in a safe place that is out of reach to avoid any accidents.

You might not want to send your papercraft at all – many of the projects in this book would also look great in a frame to be admired on a wall. If this is the case, it is best to have a frame in mind from the beginning so that you can make sure the artwork fits. There are so many options to choose from – elaborate to simple frames, coloured backgrounds or simple mounts. Be creative and think about what will look best for your home and for the artwork.

When framing, it is a good idea to secure your artwork to a backing board using an adhesive, so that it will sit in place when mounted on the wall. Choose an adhesive that isn't too wet as you don't want your artwork to warp from moisture. A spray adhesive and double-sided tape are always good options for paper projects.

When posting your artwork, make sure it is safe and secure until your recipient opens the envelope. If the card has lots of cut details, it might be a good idea to place a protective layer over your card. Try placing a sheet of copy paper over the cut-out section of your card before you place it in the envelope so that none of the small details get caught on the inside of the envelope.

# For a loved one

# MINIATURE GARDEN

What better way to share a special moment than by sitting in a blooming garden? Practise your paper-cutting skills on this easy-to-assemble miniature garden and send it to someone special. Placed in a sunny spot and watered regularly, it will brighten up any window ledge. With just a little care, your recipient can watch the cress grow and, within a couple of weeks, even enjoy a small harvest of their own.

## YOU WILL NEED

### TOOLS

- Craft knife
- Cutting mat
- Invisible tape
- Sticky tape
- Double-sided tape

### MATERIALS

- Green cardstock (approximately 200–300 gsm/120–140 lb) cut to 110 x 210 mm (4⅓ x 8⅓ inches)
- Cotton pad
- Cress seeds

**Template (see page 132)**

**1** Enlarge the template on page 132 to 100 per cent using a photocopier and loosely cut around the couple. Place the template onto the card and secure in place with invisible tape.

**2** Using a craft knife on a cutting mat, cut along the lines within the bodies. Next cut around the outside lines of the silhouette. Then carefully remove the template.

**3** Cut a strip of sticky tape the length of the card and stick it along the bottom edge with half its width overlapping the edge. Fold the tape around the card and press down firmly on the other side. This will prevent the card from soaking up water.

**4** Attach a small piece of double-sided tape to one end of the bottom edge – at the point where the card will overlap when assembled. Do not remove the protective layer on the double-sided tape – your recipient will do this when they stick the two ends together.

**5** Finally place the card flat and
seal into an envelope with one
cotton pad, one packet of cress
seeds and the instructions below.

```
To assemble your miniature garden:
1. Place the cotton pad onto a small plate, cover with
   cress seeds and water gently with the help of a
   spoon. Dab off any excess water.
2. Remove the small square piece of protective paper
   from the bottom edge of the card, bend the card
   around to form a circle and stick the ends together.
3. Stand the card on the plate so it creates a protective
   edge around the cress pad.
4. Place in a sunny place and keep moist by adding a
   few drops of water each day. The cress will start
   growing within a few days and will be ready to eat in
   about two weeks – enjoy!
```

# VARIATION

If your recipient isn't the gardening type, they can place a tealight
within the hand-holding couple instead and watch the shadows dance
on the table.

# I MISS YOU MOBILE

Whether you are in a long-distance relationship or have a friend who has moved away, this gift is a gentle reminder of how much you miss their company. Recycle old envelopes, use different lining patterns for the teardrops or choose colours that suit your mood. This paper mobile will look beautiful turning in a window or hanging from a shelf.

## YOU WILL NEED

### TOOLS

- Craft knife
- Cutting mat
- Glue stick
- Invisible tape
- Sticky tape
- Double-sided tape
- Needle

### MATERIALS

- Black or coloured cardstock (approximately 300 gsm/140 lb) cut to 150 x 100 mm (6 x 4 inches)
- Coloured paper, old envelopes or magazines (approximately 80–100 gsm/60–70 lb)
- Thread

**Templates (see page 132)**

1 Enlarge the template on page 132 to 100 per cent using a photocopier and attach the eye template to the cardstock using invisible tape.

2 Using a craft knife on a cutting mat, cut out the shapes within the eye first before cutting around the outside edge. Once the eye has been cut out, carefully remove the template.

3 Lay the teardrop templates onto your chosen paper. Either draw around the templates with a pencil and cut out the shapes with a pair of scissors, or attach the templates using invisible tape and cut them out using a craft knife. Repeat until you have 10 small and 10 large teardrops.

4 Cut four pieces of thread approximately 20 cm (8 inches) long, and line up two or three teardrops with the thread running down the centre of them.

5 Once you are happy with their spacing, carefully secure the teardrops to the thread with small pieces of tape. Then attach either a piece of double-sided tape or glue to the back of each teardrop (the side with the thread) and attach an equal-sized teardrop to hide the thread.

6 Using the pencil, mark four dots along the bottom edge of the eye, equidistant apart, and pierce them with a needle. One after another, thread the loose ends of the teardrop chains through the holes with the help of the needle, and fasten to the card with a knot so the thread doesn't slip out. Don't let the threads hang too low, otherwise they will get tangled in the envelope.

7 Finally cut a slightly longer piece of thread and attach it to the top of the eye in the same way as in step 6.

# TIP

Wind up the hanging thread and attach it to a piece of paper or card with some low-tack tape before placing it in an envelope. This will prevent the mobile from getting tangled in the post.

# Love Birds

Love birds mate for life and usually return to the same place each year to meet. They even pine for their mate when separated. This is probably why they symbolise everlasting love, care and loyalty. Love birds are the perfect way to show someone your affection; create this delicate pop-up card as a perfect little gift to say 'I love you' or give to newlyweds on their special day.

## You will need

### TOOLS
- Craft knife
- Cutting mat
- Invisible tape

### MATERIALS
- White cardstock (approximately 200–300 gsm/120–140 lb) cut to 148 x 210 mm (5¾ x 8⅓ inches)

**Template (see page 132)**

1 Enlarge the template on page 132 to 100 per cent using a photocopier. Fold the cardstock in half with the opening to your right, so that the card opens the correct way.

2 Place the template on the card with the bird's beak pointing towards the folded edge and secure with invisible tape.

3 Using a craft knife on a cutting mat, carefully cut along the lines of the template, starting with the bird. Take care not to cut the tips of the wings, tail or beak of the bird. Next cut the line of the heart, being careful not to cut the dotted line.

4 Once all the lines are cut, gently remove the template and open up the card. Using the craft knife, carefully recut any of the lines that may not have cut fully into the second layer of the card.

5 Pop the heart and birds out from the outside in. This makes the uncut edges of the heart fold forwards.

# VARIATION

Classic white is perfect for a wedding card, but for a more vibrant finish, you can attach some coloured tissue paper behind the cut-out birds that will peek through for a nice pop of colour.

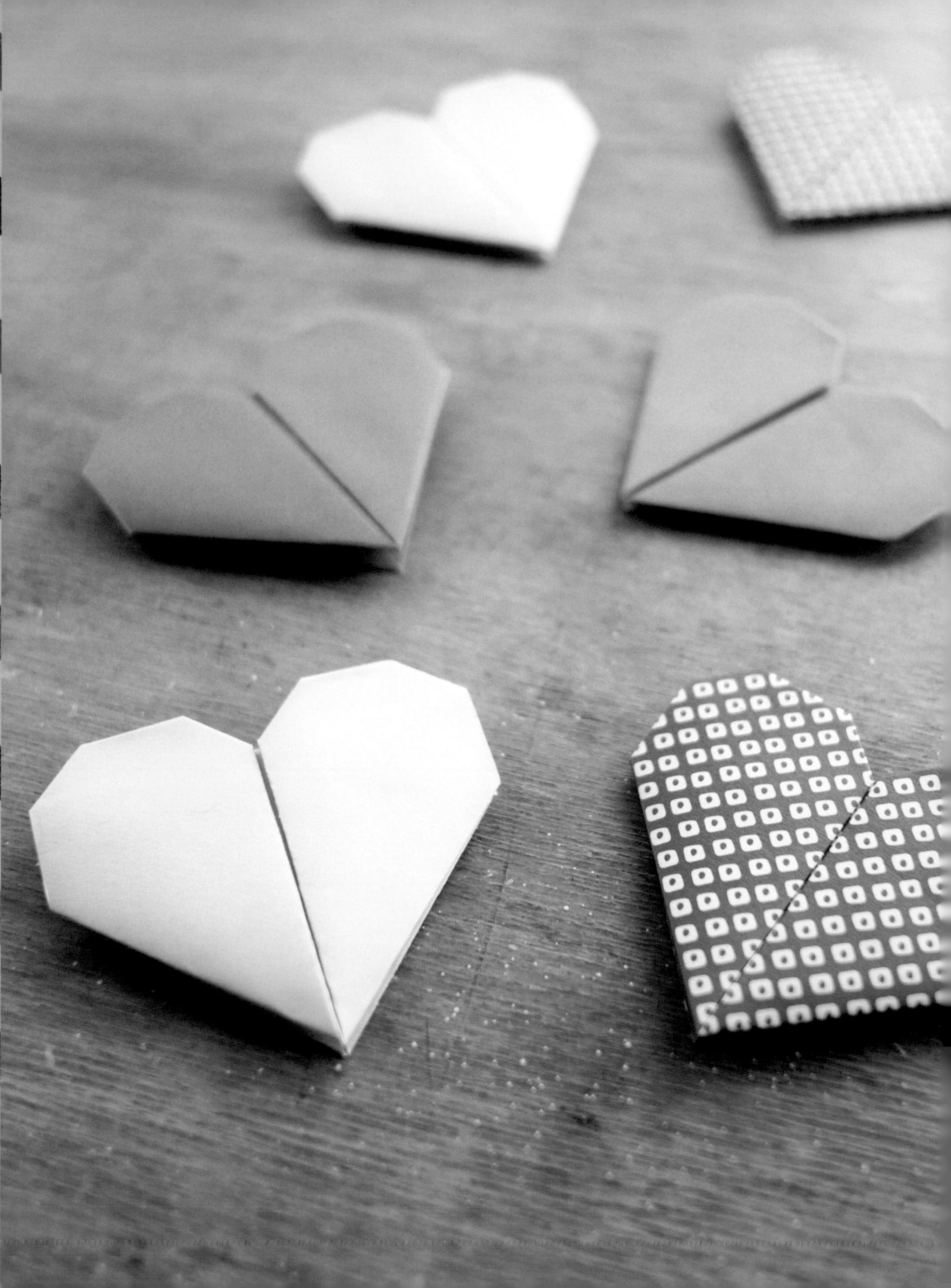

# Origami Hearts

Why not show someone how much you love them with this simple piece of origami. You could easily make a few hearts and attach them to a thin piece of string for a hanging decoration. The best thing about this project is that it requires very few materials – just select a piece of origami paper in your chosen colour and design, and you're ready to get folding.

## You will need

### MATERIALS

• Origami paper in any colour and design

1 Most origami paper has a patterned side and a plain side. If your paper has a lovely pattern, place it so the pattern is facing the table. Fold it in half horizontally and then vertically, and then unfold so you are left with the creases.

2 Next fold the bottom edge into the centre crease line. Turn the paper over and fold the bottom right-hand corner into the centre. Repeat with the left-hand corner.

3 Flip the paper over again, and this time, fold the two top corners down on themselves as shown in the image above.

4 The next step is a little tricky. Fold the top point down so that it touches the bottom point, but do so without folding the little triangles you have created on the side. Sometimes this means gently easing the paper into place.

5 Fold the two end triangles in on themselves, as shown in the image on the left.

6 Fold the edges of the two top flaps in on themselves to create a triangle from each flap. Finally fold down each of those triangles so you don't have a spiky heart. Turn the folded shape around and you have a lovely origami heart to send to someone.

# VARIATION

Origami paper is available in so many beautiful colours and often with intricately patterned designs. Why not gather together a few that complement one another in a smaller size to make lots of miniature origami hearts? You can use them to decorate a dinner table or pop in an envelope as an extra special surprise.

# Lacy Envelope Insert

The intricate design of this delicate envelope insert will really add a 'wow factor' to any simple card or handwritten note. The template for cutting the lace pattern is provided on page 133, which makes this pretty project simpler than it looks – as long as you can keep a steady hand. Give it a go and you might surprise yourself by creating a mini work of art!

## You will need

### TOOLS

- Craft knife
- Invisible tape
- Bone folder

### MATERIALS

- Coloured cardstock (approximately 170 gsm/120 lb) cut to 210 × 297 mm (8⅓ x 11¾ inches)
- Contrasting coloured paper

**Template (see page 133)**

1 Enlarge the template on page 133 to 100 per cent using a photocopier and carefully attach it to the cardstock using invisible tape. Lightly score the dotted lines on the template with a craft knife. This ensures the edges can be folded easily once cut.

2 Using a craft knife on a cutting mat, cut out the shaded areas of the template. Start with the most delicate and detailed areas of the design, so that if you make a small mistake it will not be so obvious. Work from panel to panel, completing each section as you go, and leaving the centre panel to last. If you found a particular area more difficult on a panel, start with that section on the next panel.

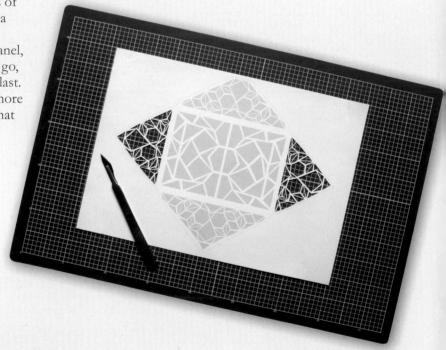

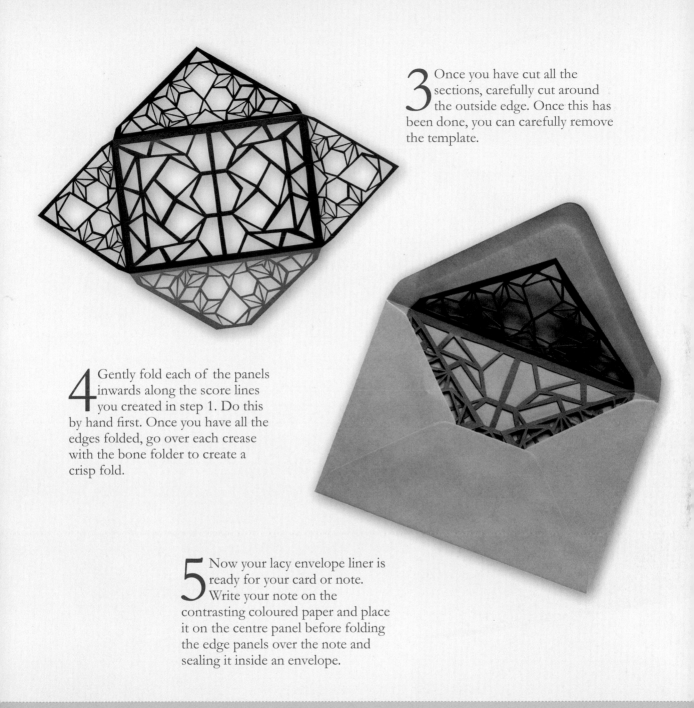

**3** Once you have cut all the sections, carefully cut around the outside edge. Once this has been done, you can carefully remove the template.

**4** Gently fold each of the panels inwards along the score lines you created in step 1. Do this by hand first. Once you have all the edges folded, go over each crease with the bone folder to create a crisp fold.

**5** Now your lacy envelope liner is ready for your card or note. Write your note on the contrasting coloured paper and place it on the centre panel before folding the edge panels over the note and sealing it inside an envelope.

# TIP

By leaving the cutting of the centre panel until last, your template will remain sturdier until the whole design is cut out.

# Stand-Up Card

Project six: Sarah Dennis

06

Want to show someone how much you care, but you're not sure how to put it in words? This beautiful circle paper-cut card speaks for itself. This stunning card is designed to sit on the windowsill where the light can shine through the circle pattern and create a delicate shadow on the window ledge.

## You Will Need

**TOOLS**

- Craft knife
- Cutting mat
- Metal ruler
- Invisible tape
- Glue stick or double-sided tape
- Scissors
- Bone folder

**MATERIALS**

- White cardstock (approximately 160 gsm/110 lb) cut to 210 x 297 mm (8⅓ x 11¾ inches)
- Blue cardstock (approximately 160 gsm/110 lb) cut to 210 x 297 mm (8⅓ x 11¾ inches)

**Templates (see page 133)**

1 Enlarge the templates on page 133 to 100 per cent using a photocopier. Place the patterned template onto the blue cardstock, matching the straight edge of the template with the edge of the cardstock. Attach using a small piece of invisible tape.

2 Using the craft knife on a cutting mat, carefully cut away the grey areas of the template. If you aren't confident using a craft knife yet, try practising some small shapes on a spare piece of paper first – this will make it easier when it comes to cutting the small areas in this design.

3 Once you have cut out all the small details, carefully remove the tape, keeping the template in place, and draw around the circle of the template. Once drawn, cut around the edge with the scissors or craft knife.

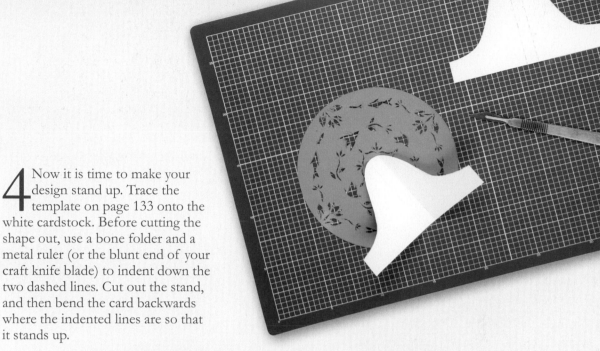

**4** Now it is time to make your design stand up. Trace the template on page 133 onto the white cardstock. Before cutting the shape out, use a bone folder and a metal ruler (or the blunt end of your craft knife blade) to indent down the two dashed lines. Cut out the stand, and then bend the card backwards where the indented lines are so that it stands up.

**5** To attach the stand to the card, add a dot of glue (or double-sided tape) to the top, line it up to the bottom of the circle and press down so it sticks. Leave to dry. Once dry, you can add a message to the back if you wish, or leave blank for a simple but effective statement.

# VARIATION

Creating your own template for this pretty shadow-casting card will open up a world of possibilities. Create a design with love heart silhouettes to give to someone you cherish, or cut out little snowflakes and holly leaves for a unique festive card.

CHAPTER TWO

02

# GIFTS BY POST

# Paper Leaf Garland

Create a unique hand-crafted garland, bringing the outdoors inside with delicate designs inspired by nature. This design comprises 12 paper leaves individually cut and folded to create beautifully intricate patterns, which are then strung on a piece of ribbon – a perfectly simple and delicate decoration for any home. Send as a house-warming gift and vary the colours according to the seasons – vibrant greens are perfect for spring, while muted browns and golds work perfectly in autumn.

## You will need

### TOOLS

- Craft knife
- Scissors
- Cutting mat
- Pencil
- Metal ruler
- Bone folder

### MATERIALS

- Cardstock in different colours (approximately 80–100 gsm/ 60–70 lb) cut to 210 x 297 mm (8⅓ x 11¾ inches), 3 sheets per garland
- Thin piece of ribbon
**Templates (see page 133)**

1 Enlarge the templates on page 133 to 100 per cent using a photocopier and cut them out. You could also sketch some of your own leaf shapes, finding inspiration in your own garden, local park or nature books.

2 Fold the coloured cardstock in half. Place the template onto the cardstock, matching up the centre line of the template to the folded edge of the cardstock. Secure the template in place and draw around it with your pencil.

3 Once you have drawn around the template, remove it carefully. Using a craft knife on a cutting mat, cut along the drawn line. Remember you will be cutting through two layers of cardstock, so take your time. Also, do not cut along the folded edge.

4 Repeat steps 2 and 3 until you have enough leaves to make a garland (I used 12 leaves in this design).

**5** Once you have all your leaves cut out, fold them in half lengthwise. Keeping your leaf folded, indent some diagonal lines onto the leaf. To do this, place a metal ruler on the leaf where you want to make a line and use a bone folder to gently indent the cardstock. Repeat until you have all the lines.

**6** Starting at the bottom of your leaf, fold the edge up along the indented line, turn the design around and then fold your leaf the opposite direction on the second indented line. Repeat this accordion fold until all the lines on the leaf have been folded. Repeat steps 5 and 6 on all of the leaves.

**7** Once each leaf has been folded, unfold all of them fully and your three-dimensional patterned leaves will be revealed.

**8** Finally create a small slit in the centre fold of your leaf about 6 mm (¼ inch) away from the edge, just large enough to fit your ribbon through. Then thread the leaves onto your ribbon by gently teasing open the slit to slide the ribbon through. Once your leaves are threaded onto the ribbon, you can easily move the leaves and space them equally – this can also be done once the garland is hanging in its recipient's house.

# TIP

To post the garland, simply place each of the leaves on top of one another neatly and seal into an envelope – this will prevent the ribbon from getting tangled in transit.

# Owl Bookmark

project eight: Marthe van Herk
08

Want to challenge your paper-cutting skills? This intricate and complex project is for you. The ancient Greeks used owls to symbolise wisdom. The goddess of wisdom, Athena, is frequently depicted as an owl, so this creature is a suitable companion for books!

## You Will Need

### TOOLS

- Craft knife
- Cutting mat
- Spray adhesive
- Invisible tape
- Bone folder

### MATERIALS

- Cardstock in three colours (approximately 160 gsm/110 lb)

**Templates (see pages 134)**

1 Enlarge the templates on page 134 to 100 per cent using a photocopier. Attach each of the templates to a different coloured cardstock using a small amount of invisible tape.

2 Using the craft knife on a cutting mat, start cutting out the detailed areas within the templates. Always start by cutting away the smallest pieces first – this preserves the strength of the template. Finish by cutting around the outer outline of the template.

3 Repeat step 2 for all card layers. Once all are cut, remove the templates.

**4** This is the moment of truth! Put the layers on top of each other and check that they fit together and if any of the layers need extra cutting. It doesn't matter if you see a little of the lower layers sticking out – this gives it extra depth and a playful effect. However, if you prefer it to look sharper, simply cut the excess away.

**5** Start gluing the layers on top of one another. Turn the top layer around and lay it flat on a protected surface. Give it a light spray with some spray adhesive and allow it to go tacky before placing the second layer on top. Repeat this with the third layer, then turn them all over to reveal your owl.

**6** Fold the branch forwards, using a bone folder to create a really sharp crease.

**7** Now it's time to send your beautiful bookmark to a book-loving friend – the owl will peer over the page they are reading and remind them of you.

## Tip

Choose a dark-coloured cardstock for the top layer to give it the best contrast. The second layer works especially well if you choose a complementary colour to the top layer. For example, if you use a dark green for the top layer, you could choose a lighter green for the second layer. The third layer is going to be the owl's eye, so a bright contrasting colour is best.

# Doves Pendant

Send someone a little love with this easy paper-cutting project – a beautiful dove pendant. The art of paper-cutting is perfect for depicting the delicate branches of a tree, so you can really show off your skills with this design. Even if you accidentally veer from the template, you can simply work the extra cut into another twist of the tree branch.

## You will need

### TOOLS

- Craft knife
- Cutting mat
- Glue
- Invisible tape

### MATERIALS

- Cardstock in white and grey (approximately 160 gsm/110 lb)
- Small piece of ribbon or string

**Templates (see page 135)**

1 Enlarge the templates on page 135 to 100 per cent using a photocopier.

2 Either trace the pendant design onto the grey cardstock or, to avoid pencil lines on your final piece, attach the template to the card using small pieces of invisible tape.

3 Using the craft knife and cutting mat, carefully cut out the pendant design. Always start by cutting away the smallest pieces first to preserve the strength of the template.

4 Repeat steps 2–3 with the dove templates and the white cardstock. If the eyes of the doves are too small to cut, you can either punch a hole with a thick needle, or simply draw them on with a marker pen.

**5** Before attaching the doves to the pendant, play around with the positioning of the birds. It gives added dimension to the pendant if you glue one on each side. Once you are happy with their position, glue the doves in place.

**6** Attach some pretty ribbon or string to hang, and wrap the pendant to send to someone deserving. Or if you can't bear to part with it, hang it in a nice spot in your own home!

# Variation

You can affix this design to a handmade card. Simply cut off the hoop at the top of the pendant and draw around the inside of the outer circle on a piece of folded cardstock. Cut out the circle shape on one side of the folded cardstock using a craft knife on a cutting mat, and stick the edges of the pendant to the rim of the hollow with a dab of glue. Voilà – you have a beautiful card!

# HANGING NOTES

These simple hanging decorations are a quick way to create something special to send by post and they are a beautiful alternative to a handwritten note. You can even make a few and string them together to create a beautiful paper garland. This project is also a great way of using up scraps of gift wrap or any other paper you have around the house.

## YOU WILL NEED

### TOOLS

- Craft knife or scissors
- Cutting mat
- Glue stick or double-sided tape
- Bone folder

### MATERIALS

- Cardstock in different colours (approximately 200–300 gsm/ 120–140 lb)
- Thin string (such as baker's twine)

**1** Gather a variety of different coloured cardstocks. Cut six circles of equal size for each hanging note, using a craft knife on a cutting mat or scissors.

**2** If you would like to write a message or note onto your circles, it is best to do it now.

**3** Fold each circle in half with the pattern or text facing inwards. Use a bone folder to create nice crisp creases.

**4** Take one folded circle and either attach a small piece of double-sided tape to one side along the folded edge, or run the glue stick along the folded edge. Carefully attach another folded circle on top so that they are stuck together. Attach another circle using the same method so that you have three stuck together.

**5** Repeat step 4 to stick the remaining three circles together. You should now have two sets of three circles stuck together. These are the two halves of your hanging note.

**6** Lay one set of three circles flat on a table and attach a piece of twine using the glue stick or double-sided tape, as shown in the photograph below. This will become your hanging loop, so make sure it is securely attached.

**7** Finally, place a piece of double-sided tape across the twine and attach the second set of three circles on top to create a full circle.

**8** Now your hanging decorations are ready to fold flat and seal into an envelope to post. When your recipient receives them, they can unflatten the decoration, hang it in their home and think of you.

# VARIATION

A fun alternative for this project is to use paper circles with a much larger circumference. The size of an average dinner plate would be a good guide. Use exactly the same step-by-step method with larger circles to create a whimsical paper lantern — great for hanging outside at a garden party.

# ENVELOPE

Many of the projects in this book need envelopes, and as some of them are not standard size you will need to create your own. A handmade envelope is the perfect finishing touch to any handmade card, and once you realise how easy it is, you'll never buy another envelope again.

## YOU WILL NEED

### TOOLS

- Craft knife
- Scissors
- Cutting mat
- Double-sided tape
- Bone folder
- Metal ruler

### MATERIALS

- Double-sided patterned paper
**Template (see page 135)**

1 Using the template on page 135 as a guide, create a template for your envelope that allows your card design to fit inside with at least 3 mm (⅛ inch) space around the edge.

2 Trace your template onto a piece of double-sided patterned paper. Cut out the envelope shape, using a craft knife on a cutting mat or scissors.

3 Score or indent the lines marked with a dashed line on the template – use a metal ruler to get nice clean, crisp score lines. Score the flap and each of the side tabs, and then score the line between your two rectangles.

4 Fold in the two side tabs and add a piece of double-sided tape to their outer edges. Remove the protective layer of the tape and press the top rectangle down on top of them to create a pouch.

5 Place your card inside the envelope and secure the flap closed using a small piece of double-sided tape, ensuring your card is nice and safe until it arrives at its final destination. You can fold the flap into the pouch instead if you don't want to glue it down.

# Paper Stamp

This is a really simple project for creating quick greetings cards or pretty personalised gift wrap. These stamps can be used again and again, and depending on how you place them, you can create many different designs. You could even create a name or initial stamp to further personalise your designs.

## You will need

### TOOLS

- Craft knife
- Cutting mat
- Pencil
- Lino cutter

### MATERIALS

- White or coloured cardstock (approximately 109 gsm/32 lb)
- Larger sheet of paper to use as gift wrap
- Ink pad in any colour
- Rubber block

**Template (see page 135)**

**1** Use a photocopier to enlarge the template on page 135 to 100 per cent, and trace the design onto the rubber block. Alternatively, draw on your own design.

**2** Using the lino cutter, cut around the outside of the design, carving away the rubber around the design so it stands out.

**3** Cut away any small details in the design, such as the central lines in the leaf, using a craft knife on a cutting mat.

**4** Now you are ready to start stamping. Turn the stamp over and press it into the ink pad. You want a nice, even coverage – not too much and not too little. Once inked, try the stamp on a scrap piece of paper first and check that you are happy with the way it looks. You can cut away some more of the rubber if you need to. Then stamp away to your heart's content, creating patterns for greetings cards or gift wrap.

## TIP

I always think it is nice to create a couple of stamps and use them both on one design for variety. Also if you want to change colour, just wipe the ink off your stamp with a damp cloth, dry and then stamp again using a new colour.

CHAPTER THREE

03

# SEND A NOTE

# BOTANICAL PAPER-CUT CARD

Create your own special, hand-crafted greetings card in a pretty paper-cut floral design. This hand-cut card is made using a simple template that you can use again and again to make as many cards as you like. The design depicts a sprig of flowers, inspired by the Astrantia plant, but feel free to design your own motif.

## YOU WILL NEED

### TOOLS

- Craft knife
- Cutting mat
- Invisible tape
- Pencil

### MATERIALS

- Yellow cardstock (approximately 200–300 gsm/120–140 lb) cut to 148 x 210 mm (5¾ x 8⅓ inches)
- Contrasting coloured paper (optional)

**Template (see page 135)**

1 Enlarge the template on page 135 to 100 per cent using a photocopier.

2 Fold the cardstock in half to create a folded card.

3 Unfold the card and attach the template to the panel on the left-hand side of the folded line using a small piece of invisible tape.

4 Using a craft knife on a cutting mat, carefully cut out the design. As there are some very fine, detailed areas, take your time. Start with the smallest sections and the stems before cutting out the flowers and leaves.

5 Once the whole design is cut out, carefully remove the template.

6 Refold the card to reveal your design. Now all you have to do is write a note inside and post it to make someone's day.

TIP

To make the design stand out even more, include a contrasting coloured-paper insert. Simply cut a piece of paper slightly smaller than your card when it's folded flat. Fold this piece of paper in half and attach it inside the card using a small piece of double-sided tape or glue.

# MESSAGE CARD

This cool card makes any occasion a special one. This project will teach you how to use paper cutting for a clever three-dimensional effect. The fine detail of the design means that the overall look of this card is understated and classy, and you can write a personal message in the banner.

## YOU WILL NEED

### TOOLS

- Craft knife
- Cutting mat
- Invisible tape
- Metal ruler
- Bone folder
- Double-sided tape or glue stick

### MATERIALS

- Coloured cardstock (approximately 170 gsm/120 lb) cut to 105 x 148 mm (4⅛ x 5⅞ inches)
- Contrasting coloured or white paper cut to 100 x 140 mm (3⅞ x 5½ inches)

**Template (see page 136)**

1 Enlarge the template on page 136 to 100 per cent using a photocopier.

2 Fold the cardstock in half to create the centre fold line. Unfold the card flat and attach the template so that the banner design is to the right of your fold line (this will be the front of your card). Secure the template in place with a small piece of invisible tape.

3 Using a craft knife on a cutting mat, cut out your design. Start by cutting the small detailed parts of the design, which in this case are the small flowers. Work your way from the inside of the design to the outside, ensuring that you cut out the small circle inside the flower before cutting out the petals.

4 Cut out the butterflies, again starting from the inside and working your way out. Start from the line on the inside of the butterfly where the head and tail begin and cut out the middle of the wing before continuing.

**5** Cut out the banners – you may find this easier to do with a ruler (use a metal ruler so the blade of the craft knife doesn't cut into the ruler as you go). Once you have cut this section out, carefully remove the template.

**6** Refold your card in half along the centre fold line and, using a bone folder, create a nice sharp crease. Fold the piece of contrasting coloured or white paper in half and place it into the centre of your card, securing it in place with some glue or a small piece of double-sided tape.

**7** For a three-dimensional look, pop out the petals and butterfly wings from the inside out. Now all that is left to do is to write your personal message in the banner sections and your card is ready to send.

# VARIATION

For a different finish, don't cut out the banners – instead cut more butterflies and flowers until they fill the whole front face of the card. If you remember to pop out every wing and petal, the overall effect will be gorgeous.

# Flower Card

Take your paper-cutting skills to the next level by adding petals and leaves to give your design a three-dimensional feel. This card is a great way to send someone flowers without the worry of them wilting!

## You will need

### TOOLS

- Craft knife
- Cutting mat
- Metal ruler
- Double-sided tape
- Invisible tape
- Glue

### MATERIALS

- Green paper and white cardstock (approximately 160 gsm/ 110 lb) cut to 210 x 297 mm (8⅓ x 11¾ inches), plus a small amount of pink, yellow and dark green cardstock of the same weight
- Cotton bud

**Templates (see page 136)**

1 Enlarge the template on page 136 to 100 per cent using a photocopier. Fold the green paper in half to form the base. Unfold the paper and lay it flat. Attach the template to the panel on the right-hand side of the folded line using a small piece of invisible tape.

2 Using a craft knife on a cutting mat, carefully cut away the grey areas of the template.

3 Cut out the petals from pink and yellow cardstock and the leaves from green – you can use the templates on page 136 or try designing some of your own. You'll need quite a lot, so cut a few extra just in case.

4 Lay your card down flat with the inside facing upwards. Add a dot of glue to the back of the flower heads. Attach three petals to each flower head – one in the centre with another petal on either side. Do the same with the stems. Leave this to dry. Be very careful not to use too much glue, as you don't want the card sticking to the table; only use enough to keep the leaves and petals in place.

**5** Once the petals are fully dry, it is time to make the flowers come to life. Using a cotton bud, gently curl the edges of the petals by rolling them around the stick. To give the flower head a more rounded look, place the top of the cotton bud on the back of the flower head and lightly pinch it until it looks curved.

**6** Use the same curling technique on the leaves to give them a more rounded look. You could even give the stems more movement by gently using your nails to add a curve to the back of the paper, in a similar way you would curl ribbon.

**7** Now add the paper insert. Fold the white card in half and trim 6 mm (¼ inch) off the sides so that it fits inside the card. Add a piece of double-sided tape to the back page of your insert – next to the fold line – and attach it to the back of your card.

**8** To ensure the flowers are secure, add a small amount of glue to the back of some of them to attach them to the white insert. Now all that is left is to write your message inside and send your creation.

# Bird Pop-Up Card

There is nothing more beautiful than giving someone a pop-up card that comes to life upon opening. The unusual triangle shape makes it extra special, while the intricate bird is sure to impress. Although this card looks complicated to make, by carefully following the instructions, you will end up with a very impressive finished card.

## You will need

### TOOLS

- Craft knife
- Cutting mat
- Metal ruler
- Permanent glue
- Invisible tape

### MATERIALS

- Yellow cardstock (approximately 200–300 gsm/120–140 lb) cut to 210 x 297 mm (8⅓ x 11¾ inches)
- Light blue, dark blue and purple cardstock (approximately 120–160 gsm/80–110 lb) cut to 210 x 297 mm (8⅓ x 11¾ inches)

**Templates (see page 136–137)**

1 Enlarge the templates on pages 136–137 to 100 per cent using a photocopier. Cut roughly around each of the templates.

2 Attach template A onto light blue cardstock with a piece of invisible tape. The rectangular shape will become the pop-up strut (see step 9).

3 Before cutting out the design, use the blunt end of your craft knife and the metal ruler to indent all the dashed lines on the template.

4 Using a craft knife on a cutting mat, carefully cut through the template and card at the same time. Cut out the smaller details on the wings first before cutting around the outside edge. Do not cut through the dashed lines.

5 Once cut out, remove the template. Now carefully fold the indented lines in the right direction as shown in the image. See the tip on the next page for more guidance.

**6** Repeat steps 3–5 for all the templates. Attach template B to the dark blue cardstock, template C to purple cardstock and template D to the yellow cardstock. Remember to cut the slit on the yellow template that is used for holding the card closed when it is finished.

**7** Time to assemble the card. Apply a small amount of glue to the bird's beak and attach it to the inside of the bird's neck. Press the neck and beak area together as if flattening the fold – this will allow the beak to position itself correctly.

**8** Turn the bird over and attach the dark blue and purple wings to the underside of the light blue wings.

**9** Next prepare the pop-up strut, which will support the bird from underneath. Fold the template for the strut along the dashed lines and glue together so that it looks like two attached hollow cubes. Make sure you have creased all the dashed lines on the strut before gluing it into place.

**10** Apply glue to the bottom of the strut and position it on the squares on the template (page 137). While the glue is still wet, close the card and make sure that it closes flat.

# TIP

If you are unsure about which way to fold, notice that there are two types of dashed lines on the template. Black dashed lines represent the Mountain Fold in the shape of an A. Green dashed lines represent the Valley Fold in the shape of a V.

# Flower Twist Card

This unusual greetings card encourages the receiver to participate. By turning the blue tab, the pattern will surprise your friend as the design comes to life. It will twist and turn and pop into a lovely flower shape. This delicate pop-up action is sure to bring a smile to the recipient's face, and the card can be displayed on a shelf or even hung on a wall for some three-dimensional art. What's more – it's quick and easy to make.

## You will need

### TOOLS

- Craft knife or scissors
- Cutting mat
- Metal ruler
- Double-sided tape
- Glue

### MATERIALS

- Orange, blue and white cardstock (approximately 200–300 gsm/ 120–140 lb)
- Yellow paper (approximately 100 gsm/65 lb) cut to 210 x 297 mm (8⅓ x 11¾ inches)

**Templates (see pages 137–138)**

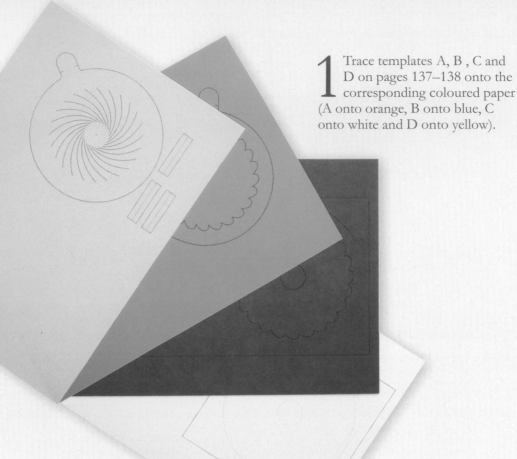

1 Trace templates A, B , C and D on pages 137–138 onto the corresponding coloured paper (A onto orange, B onto blue, C onto white and D onto yellow).

2 First cut template B out of the blue card using a craft knife on a cutting mat. Once you have cut the outside line, cut the inside line and discard the centre. Remember to cut the two small slits on the tab.

3 Next cut template D out of the yellow paper. Be very careful when cutting the lines in the centre of the design – start in the middle and cut outwards to prevent the paper slipping while you are cutting. Again, remember to cut the two small slits on the tab.

4 Apply glue to the entire underside of the blue card outline and place it on top of the yellow shape, aligning the curved edges of both pieces as carefully as you can so that the end result looks like the image on the left.

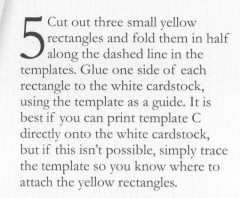

**5** Cut out three small yellow rectangles and fold them in half along the dashed line in the templates. Glue one side of each rectangle to the white cardstock, using the template as a guide. It is best if you can print template C directly onto the white cardstock, but if this isn't possible, simply trace the template so you know where to attach the yellow rectangles.

**6** Next turn the flower shape over and apply glue to the middle circle section only, where nothing is cut. Turn the flower back over and stick to the white cardstock, positioning it exactly into the traced outline and inside the folded rectangles. Cut out the orange circle and glue it to the middle of the flower.

**7** Now that the flower is ready, make the orange card in which the flower sits. Cut and fold the orange card (A) according to the template. Feed the blue tab through the slit in the orange card. Carefully apply glue to the front four edges of the white card to which the flower is attached. Align the white and orange card as well as the flower with the inner curve of the orange card and stick firmly down. Remember to let the glue dry fully before you twist the blue tab to try the pop-up on the finished card!

# Secret message Petal Card

This beautiful card is the perfect introduction to the art of paper-cutting and includes an exciting element of interaction for the receiver. Simply peel each petal back and place into the pre-cut slots to reveal a hidden message around the edge and a contrasting colour in the centre of the flower. They say a flower can speak a thousand words and this card is no exception. Perfect for thank you cards, birth announcements, invitations, love letters or just to say hello.

## You will need

### TOOLS

- Craft knife
- Cutting mat
- Metal ruler
- Double-sided tape or glue
- Pen and pencil

### MATERIALS

- White cardstock (approximately 160–300 gsm/90 lb index–100 lb cover) cut to 160 x 320 mm (6 x 12 inches)
- Light blue and bright orange paper (approximately 90 gsm/60 lb) cut to 210 x 297 mm (8⅓ x 11¾ inches)

**Template (see page 138)**

1 Stick together two pieces of
coloured paper to make a piece
of paper that is blue on one side
and orange on the other. Print or
trace the template on page 138 onto
the blue side and then cut out the
square outline by lining up a metal
ruler along each straight edge and
cutting with a craft knife on a
cutting mat.

2 Now cut out the flower design.
Make sure that the little slots in
the middle are accurate and that
the holes don't touch each other. The
slots are for the cut-out flower petals.
A good tip is to cut the short vertical
lines first, then cut the width of
the slots.

4 Peel off the double-sided tape from the cut-out flower square and stick it onto the front of the white card. Now you need to write in the message, one letter under each petal. You have 12 petals, which equals 12 letters, so plan accordingly. Lift each petal carefully to write the letter underneath, making sure that you don't bend the paper too much. Don't forget to provide the instructions to the recipient on the back of the card so they know to fold back each petal and place each tip into the centre slots to reveal your hidden message.

3 Turn over and apply glue or thin strips of double-sided tape all around the orange side of the card. Make sure that the glued area is only on the edges of the card, so it doesn't interfere with the shape of the cut-out flower. Take the white cardstock, score down the middle and fold it in half to make a square card.

# PIGEON POSTCARD

Homing pigeons have long been used to carry messages over long distances. Why not send this series of postcards, one at a time, to keep a friend or loved one up to date with your holiday plans or to get them through difficult times? You can send your composite postcards daily or weekly and decide for yourself how far your homing pigeon should travel across the map by varying the length and number of cards.

## YOU WILL NEED

### TOOLS

- Craft knife
- Cutting mat
- Scissors
- Ruler and pen
- Glue stick
- Invisible tape
- Sticky tape
- Double-sided tape

### MATERIALS

- Four pieces of cream cardstock (approximately 350 gsm/130 lb) cut to 102 x 152 mm (6 x 4 inches)
- Black paper 210 x 148 mm (8⅓ x 5¾ inches)
- A map

**Template (see page 139)**

1 On one side of each piece of cream cardstock, use a ruler and pen to mark a centre line and four parallel lines on the lower part of the right-hand side. You will later write your recipient's address here and your message on the left side of the card.

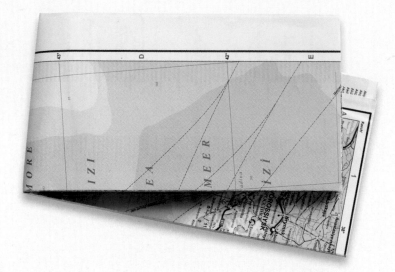

2 Select an area of the map measuring approximately 13 x 65 cm (5 x 25 inches), marking out the area with a pencil. Using scissors, cut out the section of the map along your pencil markings, turn the map over and stick the pieces of card across the back. Start at one end and join them up seamlessly in a straight line. Make sure to glue all the way to the edge of each card and press down firmly.

3 Cut away the surplus map around the cards and carefully separate them from each other. The map should run continuously across all four cards. Check all edges and corners in case they need a little extra glue to keep them stuck together.

4 Enlarge the template on page 139 to 100 per cent using a photocopier, and stick the template onto a sheet of black paper.

5 With a sharp pair of scissors, cut around each element roughly first. This makes it easier to cut along the delicate lines with more precision. For fine details or elements that cannot be reached with scissors, use a craft knife on a cutting mat. Hold the card down with one hand and with the other carefully guide the craft knife along the lines.

6 Lay out the postcards so that the sections of the map line up in the correct order. Glue down the silhouetted figures to the edges of the first and last cards, and then decide the flight path of the pigeons and glue them down firmly. If you decide to use more than four cards, you could spread the pigeons out to have one per card or cut more than one of the same shape and vary the sequence and positioning.

# VARIATION

You can also use pre-printed postcards and glue your map across the image area; or leave off the map altogether and have the birds fly across postcards showing land or city scapes. This might be a nice way to include views of your holiday destination.

# A MESSAGE IN AN ENVELOPE

# SENDING SPRING

This project is perfect for those who live where it seems as though winter will never end and spring will never arrive. It's up to you to create some spring joy and send it to others who are in desperate need of some colour to warm up the last months of winter. Their day is guaranteed to brighten when they open the envelope and spring confetti spills out.

## YOU WILL NEED

### TOOLS

- Invisible tape
- Craft knife or scissors
- Cutting mat
- Glue stick
- Hole punch

### MATERIALS

- Cardstock in a variety of spring colours (approximately 200–300 gsm/120–140 lb)
- Envelope
**Templates (see page 139)**

1 Enlarge the templates on page 139 to 100 per cent using a photocopier.

2 Cut out the templates and trace them onto your chosen cardstock, or attach the templates with invisible tape. Cut out the grass, stems and flower petals – or better yet, design some spring flowers of your own.

3 Attach the petals to the stems with glue to create flower shapes – make sure you glue petals to both sides to hide the stem joins.

4 Use a hole punch to cut out the centres of some flowers, as indicated in the flower templates. Retain the punched circles, as these can be added to the envelope to create extra confetti.

5 Once you have a nice bunch of flowers and grasses, fill an envelope with your creations.

6 Finally, slip a little note into the envelope, or send anonymously for even more of a surprise.

# VARIATION

Once you have created your flowers and grasses, you can attach a few of them to the front of a card to create a simple but beautiful floral bouquet.

# Blue Ribbon Thank You

**21**

This card is the perfect 'thank you' to send to friends after they have hosted a dinner party. Customise your card by adding an award category, such as 'Best Sunday Brunch', or 'Winner: Most Delicious Chocolate Cake'. What a lovley way to tell them that their meal was great! To make this project even more special, design your own food items based on what they served. A sure way to guarantee a second dinner invitation...

## You will need

### TOOLS

- Craft knife or scissors
- Cutting mat
- Invisible tape
- Glue stick or double-sided tape
- Metal ruler

### MATERIALS

- White or cream cardstock (approximately 200–300 gsm/ 120–140 lb), cut to 127 x 178 mm (5 x 7 inches) and folded in half
- White cardstock or watercolour paper (approximately 300 gsm/ 140 lb)
- Blue coloured paper (approximately 160 gsm/110 lb)
- Paper napkin
- Miscellaneous coloured paper
- Paints or coloured markers
- Sewing pin (optional)

**Templates (see page 140)**

1 Enlarge the templates on page 140 to 100 per cent using a photocopier. Roughly cut around each template.

2 Place the ribbon templates onto the blue paper, and either trace around them with a pencil, or attach them to the blue paper with invisible tape. Cut out the ribbons using a metal ruler and a craft knife on a cutting mat. Attach the two smaller ribbons to the large ribbon using a small piece of double-sided tape.

3 Using the circular template, either trace it or attach it to the white cardstock and cut around it. This will be the plate – you may wish to decorate it to make it look more like a plate. Use paints or markers to add some detail – such as a single blue line or geometric pattern.

4 Cut two long strips from the paper napkin, approximately 25 x 230 mm (1 x 9 inches). Glue the strips together to create one long strip.

5 Take one of the narrow ends of the strip and fold it over about 6 mm (¼ inch). Repeat this process backwards and forwards to create an accordion – fold along entire length of the strip.

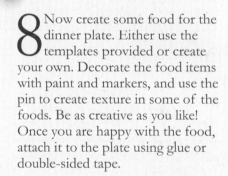

6 Once folded, attach the two end pieces together using either a small piece of double-sided tape or a glue stick so that the strip begins to resemble a rosette.

7 Attach the paper ribbons to the back of the rosette with a small piece of tape. Then secure the rosette to the back of the plate with more pieces of tape (this won't be seen from the front so you don't have to be too neat).

8 Now create some food for the dinner plate. Either use the templates provided or create your own. Decorate the food items with paint and markers, and use the pin to create texture in some of the foods. Be as creative as you like! Once you are happy with the food, attach it to the plate using glue or double-sided tape.

9 Finally, attach the ribbon to the outside of the folded cardstock using a piece of double-sided tape or glue, and write a personal thank-you note inside.

# FLORAL BORDER NOTECARD

Create a delicate floral border to dress a letter to a loved one or to create a beautiful 'thank you' note. You could also turn the floral border into a frame by adding a photograph or artwork to the centre panel for a truly personal gift. This design is so versatile that I am sure you will use it again and again.

## YOU WILL NEED

### TOOLS

- Craft knife
- Cutting mat
- Metal ruler
- Invisible tape
- Glue stick or double-sided tape

### MATERIALS

- Coloured cardstock (approximately 200–300 gsm/120–140 lb)
- White or contrasting paper (optional)

**Template (see page 140)**

1 Enlarge the template on page 140 to 100 per cent using a photocopier.

2 Cut out a piece of cardstock that is slightly larger than the template. Attach the template to the card using a couple of pieces of invisible tape.

3 Using a craft knife on a cutting mat, carefully start cutting out the white sections of the template. Cut out the small details within the design before cutting the outside edge to ensure the template doesn't move while you are cutting.

4 Once all the white sections are cut out, carefully remove the template.

**5** You can either write directly on the centre of the design or you can create a separate panel to stick on your design. To do this, cut a rectangle of white or contrasting paper (lighter in colour so you can write on it) that is slightly smaller than the inside panel of your design.

**6** Use either a small piece of double-sided tape or a glue stick to attach the paper panel to the centre of your design.

**7** Now all that is left is to write your note of thanks or love to the recipient.

# VARIATION

This design can also double as beautiful tableware for a sophisticated gathering. Enlarge the design, match the colour to your theme, and suddenly you have stunning hand-crafted place mats to adorn your table.

# Patterned Gatefold Card

project twenty three: Emily Hogarth

23

The gold paper in this card adds a special sparkle that will make anyone's day. This card opens from the middle, so it also makes a great invitation to a dinner party or a menu holder — all you have to do is print the party details or menu and attach it to the inside of the card.

## You will need

### TOOLS

- Craft knife
- Cutting mat
- Metal ruler
- Invisible tape
- Spray adhesive
- Glue stick or double-sided tape
- Pencil

### MATERIALS

- Black cardstock (approximately 200–300 gsm/120–140 lb)
- Gold paper in two contrasting shades

**Template (see page 140)**

**1** Enlarge the template on page 140 to 100 per cent using a photocopier. Cut out a piece of cardstock that is the same height as your template and six times the width.

**2** Divide the cardstock into three sections and mark with a pencil line. Each third should measure twice the width of your template.

**3** Fold the gatefold card in on itself, scoring down the pencil lines. Then fold each of these end sections in half again to create the basic structure of your card. It is best to fold the card before you cut the pattern so the card will fold into place easily at the end.

**4** Unfold the card and use invisible tape to attach the templates to the panels on either side of the wide centre panel.

**5** Using a craft knife on a cutting mat, cut out the white areas on the templates, pushing through to remove them from the card at the same time. Once all the white areas have been cut, carefully remove the templates.

6 Now add a contrasting coloured paper to the back of the cut sections of card. To do this, cut two pieces of paper a little smaller than the template size. Spray the backs of the two cut-out panels with spray adhesive, but be very careful to avoid spraying the rest of the card – you only want the cut-out panel to be sticky.

7 Once sprayed carefully lay the contrasting paper on top of the cut-out panel. Turn it over to see the effect. At this stage, if you want to add a secondary colour, use a craft knife on a cutting mat to cut out some of the triangles and diamonds from your contrasting paper, then use the same method to add another coloured paper behind it.

8 Next attach a couple of pieces of double-sided tape (or use a glue stick) to the two end panels of your card and fold them in on themselves, covering the contrasting papers. Press down firmly to secure them in place.

9 Finally, fold the end panels in on themselves again so they meet in the middle to create your gatefold card.

# WHALE CARD

This card is perfect for someone about to embark on a journey. In good and bad times, this card will reach out to someone and show them how much you care. This simple but effective design uses positive and negative space to create a striking design.

## YOU WILL NEED

### TOOLS

- Craft knife and blades
- Scissors
- Cutting mat
- Glue stick or double-sided tape
- Invisible tape
- Metal ruler
- Bone folder

### MATERIALS

- White cardstock (approximately 160 gsm/110 lb) cut to 210 x 297 mm (8⅓ x 11¾ inches)
- Dark blue cardstock (approximately 160 gsm/110 lb) cut to 210 x 297 mm (8⅓ x 11¾ inches)

**Templates (see page 141)**

1 Enlarge the templates on page 141 to 100 per cent using a photocopier. Before attaching the whale design template to white cardstock, cut around the outside edge. Line up the template with the bottom edge of the white cardstock and attach it with a small piece of invisible tape.

2 Cut away all the shaded areas on your template using a craft knife on a cutting mat.

3 Before removing the template, place a metal ruler along the dotted line and indent the line with a bone folder or the blunt side of your craft knife to create the fold of your card. Once this is done, you can draw around the outside of your template with a pencil and cut the card out.

4 Now add the inner cardstock. Cut out a circle of white, then a circle of dark blue cardstock using the templates provided on page 141. These should fit inside your cut-out card.

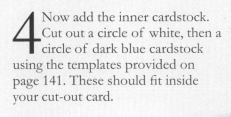

5 Attach double-sided tape or a dab of glue to the top horizontal line of the white cardstock. Line this up with the indented line inside so the card is on the back side; this is the side where you will write your message.

6 Lastly, use glue or double-sided tape to attach the blue cardstock to the underside of your paper-cut card so that it shows through at the front. Now your beautiful card is ready to have a message written inside.

# PARROTS

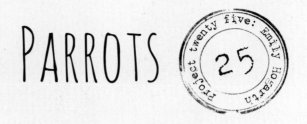

project twenty five: Emily Hogarth

25

Carrier pigeons have been used as delivery birds for a very long time. They always know where their home is and often fly with a little note carried on their leg. Create a colourful interpretation of the carrier pigeon in this flying parrot card. It would also make a great kids' party invitation (see variation).

## YOU WILL NEED

### TOOLS

- Craft knife
- Cutting mat
- Invisible tape
- Glue stick or double-sided tape

### MATERIALS

- Cardstock in three colours (approximately 200–300 gsm/ 120–140 lb)
- Brass paper fasteners

**Templates (see page 141)**

1 Enlarge the templates on page 141 to 100 per cent using a photocopier. Cut roughly around each template, so they can be attached to different coloured papers.

2 Attach the templates for the main body and top wing feather to one of the coloured papers using invisible tape. Attach the templates for the beak, middle wing feather and top tail feather to the second sheet of coloured paper, and the templates for the eye, bottom wing feather and bottom tail feather to the third sheet.

3 Using a craft knife on a cutting mat, cut out any small details within the templates and then cut around the outside edge. Repeat this for all the pieces. Make sure you store all the pieces safely as you work, as it can be very easy to misplace a small eye, for example. Cut the two small crosses on the top wing layer and the main body where the wing will be fastened to the main body.

4 Start putting the sections of your bird together. Attach small pieces of double-sided tape (or use a glue stick) to the backs of the tail feathers and carefully place each one onto the main bird body. Attach the two beak pieces and the eye to the main body, and then attach the wing feathers to the back of the main wing.

5 Once the bird body and wing are finished, you want to attach them together. Roughly align the two crosses you made in the wing and body, and use a craft knife to cut through the extra layers on the wing.

6 Next gently push the brass fastener so that it goes all the way through the wing and the body. Turn the whole bird over, and gently bend the arms of the fastener.

7 Now that your wing is attached, you can write a little message under the wing on the main body of the bird and swing the wing back into place. When your recipient receives the bird and lifts the wing, your message will be revealed.

# VARIATION

These birds make great kids' pirate party invitations. Add a little eye patch and hat to each parrot for even more fun!

# Templates

## Love Birds: page 36 { shown at 50% }

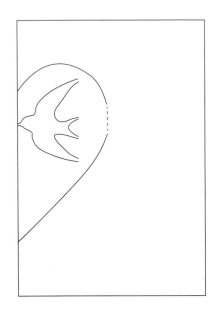

## Miniature Garden: page 28

{ shown at 50% }

## I Miss You Mobile: page 33 { shown at 50% }

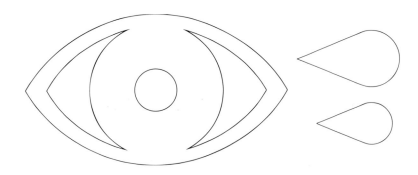

# Lacy Envelope Insert: page 44
{ shown at 50% }

# Stand-Up Card: page 49 { shown at 50% }

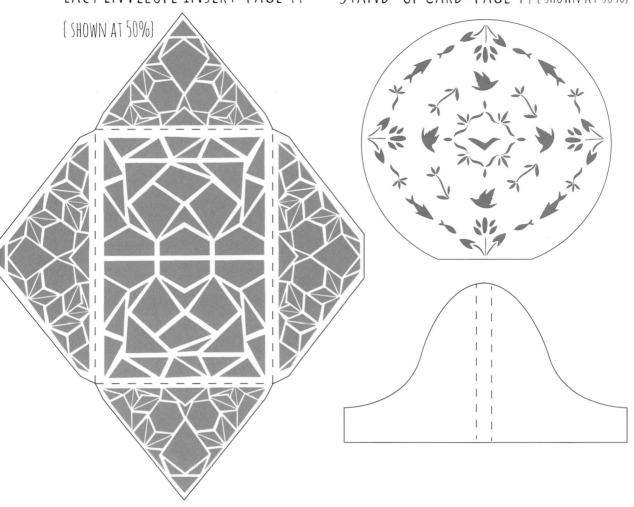

# Paper Leaf Garland: page 54 { shown at 50% }

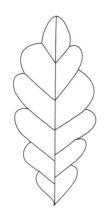

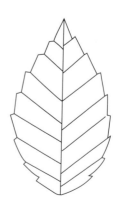

# Owl Bookmark: page 59
## Layer 1

# Owl Bookmark Layer 2 [ shown at 50% ]

## Owl Bookmark Layer 3 [ shown at 50% ]

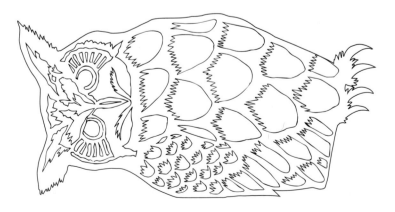

# Doves Pendant: page 62

[ shown at 50% ]

# Paper Stamp: page 73 [ shown at 80% ]

# Botanical Paper-Cut Card: page 78

[ shown at 80% ]

# Envelope: page 70 [ shown at 50% ]

## Message Card: page 83 { shown at 50% }

## Flower Card: page 86 { shown at 50% }

## Bird Pop-Up Card: page 91
{ shown at 50% } A

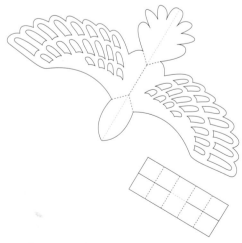

## Bird Pop-Up Card: page 91 { shown at 50% } B

# Bird Pop-Up Card: page 91
{ shown at 50% } C

# Bird Pop-Up Card: page 91
{ shown at 50% } D

# Flower Twist Card: Page 94 { shown at 50% } A

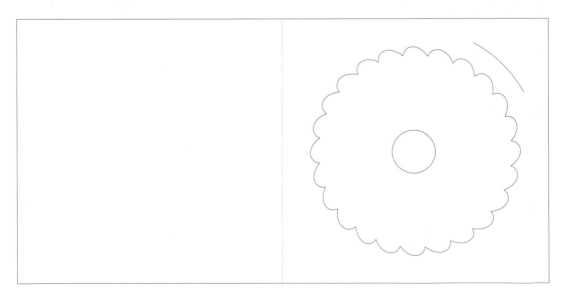

## Flower Twist Card: Page 94

{ shown at 50% } B

## Flower Twist Card: Page 94

{ shown at 50% } C

## Flower Twist Card: Page 94

{ shown at 50% } D

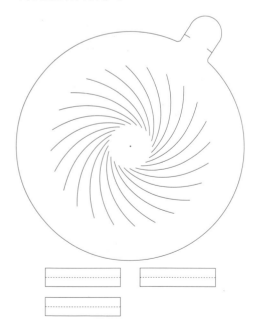

## Secret Message Petal Card: page 99

{ shown at 50% }

# Pigeon Postcard: page 102 [ shown at 80% ]

# Sending Spring: page 108 [ shown at 50% ]

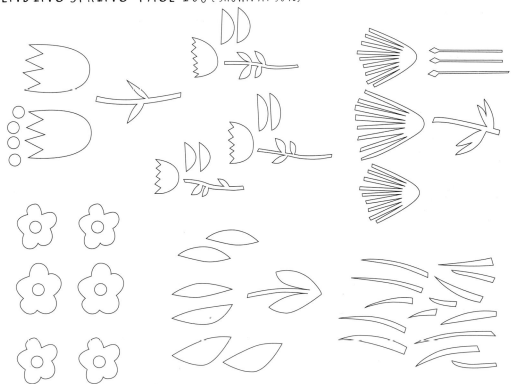

# Blue Ribbon Thank You: PAGE 113 { SHOWN AT 80%}

## Floral Border Notecard: PAGE 116 { SHOWN AT 50%}

## Patterned Gatefold Card: PAGE 121
{ SHOWN AT 50%}

# Whale Card: page 124 { shown at 50% }

# Parrots: page 129
{ shown at 50% }

# About the Author

**EMILY HOGARTH** is a paper-cut illustrator living and working in Edinburgh. She works with paper everyday and, with the aid of a scalpel, transforms simple pieces of paper into delicate and treasured works of art. Through her motto, *making the everyday magical*, Emily tries to capture the magic of her surroundings and translate them into pretty patterned illustrations and prints. Emily's relationship with paper started while she was studying textile design at Edinburgh College of Art. She found paper cutting was a quick way of creating sharp, bold and uniquely individual stencils for screen printing. She went on to study for an MA in textiles, where she refined her paper-cutting skills as well as her knowledge of illustration and graphic design. Today she runs her own illustrating business, www.emilyhogarth.com, and exhibits her artwork throughout the UK.

## About the Contributors

**IVANA CHARVATOVA AND OTOKAR CHARVAT** are siblings who, from a young age, have dreamt of running a creative design venture together. After resigning as a teacher of woodcarving at the School of Applied Art in Prague, Otokar started his own company, designing innovative furniture. Ivana had for many years developed her expertise in novelty book packaging and decided to join Otokar in business. Together they now create 3D interactive objects, such as paper models, pop-ups, boxes, novelty books and greetings cards. Paperspirala is Ivana and Otokar's new creative design studio based in London, UK – visit www.paperspirala.blogspot.co.uk and www.paperspirala.com.

**SARAH DENNIS** completed a foundation course in art and design at Brighton City College, followed by a degree in illustration at the University of the West of England. Her work combines traditional *scherenschnitte* (paper cutting) with collage. Inspired by the beauty of nature in fairy tales and whimsical childhood dreams, she tells classic poems and folk tales through the medium of paper. Each piece she makes is hand-cut using a craft knife to reveal exquisite detail. Sarah currently works as a full-time artist and illustrator in Bristol. Not limiting herself to any one type of project, she takes on a variety of work and welcomes individual requests for bespoke, hand-crafted artwork. To learn more visit www.sarah-dennis.co.uk.

**LYNN HATZIUS** is an illustrator, collage artist and printmaker originally from Germany. She came to London to study illustration and fine-art printmaking, and now has 10 years' experience as a freelance creative. Most of her commissioned work is in publishing, designing book covers for clients including: Random House, Bloomsbury, Pan Macmillan and Simon & Schuster. Her illustrations have also appeared in publications such as *The Guardian*, *The Times* and BBC magazines, as well as on a number of record sleeves. Through her explorations in printmaking and collage, she continuously develops personal projects and regularly exhibits her work. See examples of her work at www.lynnhatzius.com.

**EMILY ISABELLA** is one-part designer, one-part illustrator and one-part dreamer. Together, these elements make up her studio, Emily Isabella Illustration and Design, based in the beautiful Hudson Valley – just north of NYC. As a child, Emily wandered her family's Wisconsin prairie, pressing Queen Anne's Lace flowers against her cheeks, pretending they were powder brushes. Her work reflects this idealism and serves as a reminder to continue to tap into our imaginations and remember the children we still are. You can see more of her work at www.emilyisabella.com.

**FREYA LINES** is a designer and craftsperson based in London. She finds inspiration in all things paper and nature, particularly leaves, seeds and flowers. Freya creates hand-illustrated surface designs, decorating homewares, accessories and stationery, along with bespoke paper-crafted works. Since graduating from the University of the Arts London in 2010, Freya has worked on various commissions for different clients; from greetings cards to branding, logo and website illustration. She also creates bespoke handmade paper-cut works from album cover artwork to hand-crafted wedding table decorations. Visit www.linesdesigns.co.uk.

**MARTHE VAN HERK** graduated from University of the Arts, Utrecht as an art teacher. After a few years of teaching, Marthe felt an irresistible urge to revisit her own creative work. She was inspired to try paper cutting by the work of Dutch artist Geertje Aalders and went on to develop her own style of incredibly delicate and intricate pictures. Her shop, Whispering Paper is the product of countless hours spent honing the drawing and cutting skills required to produce this beautiful and fragile art form. View Marthe's work at www.facebook.com/WhisperingPaper and www.etsy.com/shop/WhisperingPaper.

**MR YEN** also known as Jonathan Chapman, creates hand-cut and laser-cut art, designs and greetings cards. With four years' experience as a paper-cut artist, he has worked with clients such as *The Oprah Magazine* to create delicate and dramatic designs. Mr Yen is based in Yorkshire in the UK and is available to create custom pieces for all occasions. Visit www.mr-yen.com to learn more.

# INDEX

Page numbers in **bold** type refer to templates.